WELCOME TO MY COUNTRY

Welcome to
INDONESIA

Gareth Stevens Publishing
A WORLD ALMANAC EDUCATION GROUP COMPANY

Written by
GERALDINE MESENAS/FREDERICK FISHER

Designed by
HASNAH MOHD ESA

Picture research by
SUSAN JANE MANUEL

First published in North America in 2001 by
Gareth Stevens Publishing
A World Almanac Education Group Company
330 West Olive Street, Suite 100
Milwaukee, Wisconsin 53212 USA

For a free color catalog describing
Gareth Stevens' list of high-quality books
and multimedia programs, call
1-800-542-2595 (USA) or
1-800-461-9120 (CANADA).
Gareth Stevens Publishing's
Fax: (414) 332-3567.

© **TIMES EDITIONS PTE LTD 2001**
Originated and designed by
Times Editions
An imprint of Times Media Private Limited
A member of the Times Publishing Group
Times Centre, 1 New Industrial Road
Singapore 536196
http://www.timesone.com.sg/te

Library of Congress Cataloging-in-Publication Data
Mesenas, Geraldine.
Welcome to Indonesia / Geraldine Mesenas and Frederick Fisher.
p. cm. — (Welcome to my country)
Includes bibliographical references and index.
ISBN 0-8368-2517-9 (lib. bdg.)
1. Indonesia—Juvenile literature. [1. Indonesia]
I. Fisher, Frederick. II. Title. III. Series
DS615.M46   2001
959.8—dc21   00-057349

PICTURE CREDITS
A.N.A. Press Agency: 4
Archive Photos: 15 (bottom), 16, 34
Bes Stock: 33, 35, 38, 39, 45
Michele Burgess: 3 (top), 21, 22, 25, 26,
    27, 31, 32 (bottom)
Focus Team/Italy: 23
Jill Gocher: 8
HBL Network: 5, 14, 32 (top)
The Hutchison Library: 2, 3 (bottom), 7,
    20, 41
International Photobank: 18, 30
Bjorn Klingwall: 3 (center), 24, 37
Earl and Nazima Kowall: 9 (bottom), 40
Richard l'Anson: cover, 1
Christine Osborne Pictures: 29
Photobank Photolibrary: 9 (top), 10, 11
The Straits Times: 13, 36 (both)
Topham Picturepoint: 12, 15 (top
    and center)
Travel Ink: 6
Nik Wheeler: 17, 19, 28

Digital Scanning by Superskill Graphics Pte Ltd

Printed in Malaysia

1 2 3 4 5 6 7 8 9 05 04 03 02 01

Contents

Words that appear in the glossary are printed in **boldface** type the first time they occur in the text.

Welcome to Indonesia!

Indonesia is the largest country in Southeast Asia. From tropical rain forests to towering skyscrapers, it is a blend of natural wonders and modern buildings. Let's learn about Indonesia's amazing culture and people!

Opposite: The costumes worn for many traditional Indonesian dances are very elaborate.

Below: The *bajaj* (BAH-jaj) is a common sight on the streets of Jakarta.

The Flag of Indonesia

The Indonesian flag is half red and half white. The red band stands for courage and freedom. The white band stands for justice and purity. This flag was officially adopted in 1949, four years after the country became independent.

The Land

The Indonesian **archipelago** has over thirteen thousand islands. The larger islands include Borneo, Celebes, Java, the Moluccas, New Guinea, and Sumatra. Indonesia shares the island of Borneo with the Kingdom of Brunei

Below: Mount Sinabung, located on the island of Sumatra, is one of Indonesia's active volcanoes.

and two Malaysian states, Sabah and Sarawak. It also shares the island of New Guinea with Papua New Guinea. Indonesia's capital city, Jakarta, is on the island of Java.

Natural Wonders and Disasters

With its thousands of islands, Indonesia has a lot of beaches, which attract many tourists. The fascinating sea life around the islands attracts divers and snorkelers. Along with Indonesia's natural wonders, however, come natural disasters, such as volcanic eruptions and earthquakes. In 1992, the Flores earthquake killed over two thousand people.

Left: Indonesia's most beautiful beaches are found on the island of Bali.

Climate

Indonesia lies along the equator, so it has a tropical climate. **Monsoon** rains fall from November to March. During this wet season, the heaviest rains fall in large areas of eastern Sumatra, southern Borneo, and Java. During the dry season, which lasts from June to October, very little rain falls. The rain forests become extremely dry, and forest fires occur often.

Above:
This Indonesian girl shows how useful a banana leaf can be during a heavy downpour.

Plants and Animals

Indonesia's forests are filled with ferns, mosses, vines, and giant trees. Some of the trees grow to be 200 feet (61 meters) tall. The rain forests also have many different kinds of native flowers, including dozens of different orchids.

Above: The giant *Rafflesia arnoldii* is the largest flower in the world. It can be found in the jungles of Sumatra and Borneo.

Many species of mammals, reptiles, birds, and insects live in the Indonesian rain forest. Apes and monkeys can be found on most of the islands. Jungle cats, such as tigers and leopards, live on the larger islands.

Left: Komodo dragons roam the island of Komodo. They can grow to be 10 feet (3 m) long.

History

Many kingdoms ruled Indonesia over the centuries, from the Sailendra and the Mataram dynasties in the ninth century to the Majapahit kingdom, which came to power in the late thirteenth century.

Spice trading, which attracted Muslim traders from the Middle East, led to the spread of Islam throughout much of Indonesia. By the 1500s, the Portuguese, British, and Dutch had arrived, too. They all wanted to control the spice trade.

Below: The Prambanan temple complex was built by the rulers of the Mataram dynasty.

The Dutch East India Company came to Indonesia in 1602. By 1619, the Dutch had made Jakarta their capital. When the Dutch East India Company went bankrupt in 1800, the Dutch government took control of its Indonesian territories. All of Indonesia became a Dutch colony by the end of the nineteenth century.

In the 1900s, the Dutch introduced the Ethical Policy, which provided money to develop agriculture, health, and education systems in Indonesia.

Above: During Dutch colonial rule, the Dutch people lived in luxury. They had large houses and employed many Indonesian servants.

Sukarno and Independence

In 1927, an Indonesian named Sukarno formed the Indonesian Nationalist Party (PNI). The Dutch, however, arrested Sukarno for his political activities. During World War II, Sukarno helped the Japanese invade Indonesia and drive out the Dutch. When the war ended in 1945, Sukarno declared Indonesia's independence and became president.

Left: Queen Juliana of the Netherlands signed the act that finally granted Indonesia full independence on December 27, 1949.

Indonesia under Suharto

As president, Sukarno dissolved all political parties and the elected parliament. He did not maintain good relations with the United States and other Western powers. In 1966, an army general named Suharto made Sukarno resign. Suharto took over control of the country. He was on friendly terms with the Western powers and resolved conflicts with Malaysia. He also played a key role in forming the Association of Southeast Asian Nations (ASEAN).

Above: Suharto (*second from left*) met with leaders from five other ASEAN nations — Brunei, Malaysia, the Philippines, Singapore, and Thailand — in 1992.

Economic Crisis

In 1997, the Southeast Asian economy experienced a major **recession**. As poverty and unemployment increased, Suharto and his family members were accused of being **corrupt**. Riots broke out in Jakarta and Medan in May 1998, and hundreds were killed. Foreign **investors** fled the country, and on May 21, 1998, Suharto resigned.

Below: In May 1998, Indonesian students held frequent demonstrations to show their unhappiness with the government.

Sukarno (1901–1970)

In 1945, Sukarno declared Indonesia's independence and became its first president. He was practically a **dictator** from 1959 to 1965. In 1966, Suharto **ousted** him from office.

Sukarno

Mohammad Hatta (1902–1980)

Mohammad Hatta was Indonesia's vice-president under Sukarno. In 1948, he became prime minister. In 1956, Hatta resigned because he disagreed with Sukarno's policies. He returned to politics, however, after Sukarno left office.

Mohammad Hatta

Megawati Sukarnoputri (1947–)

Sukarno's daughter, Megawati Sukarnoputri, is the leader of the Indonesian Democratic Party (PDI). During the elections of 1999, Sukarnoputri became vice-president of Indonesia.

Megawati Sukarnoputri

Government and the Economy

Indonesia is a **constitutional republic** with three government divisions. The president leads the executive branch for a five-year term. The legislative branch, which is called the People's Consultative Assembly, elects the

Left: When former Indonesian president Suharto (*right*) retired in May 1998, he was replaced by Jusuf Habibie (*left*). Abdurrahman Wahid was elected president of Indonesia in 1999.

president. The assembly also decides government policies and approves all laws. It has 400 elected members and 100 appointed members, plus 500 other legislators. Assembly members represent groups, such as farmers, educators, business people, and women, as well as certain areas of the country.

The judicial branch conducts civil and criminal cases in district courts. Fourteen major cities have high courts. The supreme court in Jakarta is the highest court of appeal.

Left: In Indonesia, the president is in charge of the armed forces.

Economy

More than half of Indonesia's workforce is employed in agriculture. Major crops include rice, corn, sweet potatoes, sugarcane, coffee, tea, and tobacco. Still, many food items are imported from other countries.

Fishing is also an important industry in Indonesia. This island country has an abundance of sea products. Thousands of tons of fish, pearls, and shells are harvested every year.

Below: These women are harvesting rice, one of Indonesia's main crops.

The Indonesian government has encouraged the development of manufacturing, too. These industries include petroleum refining, textiles, food processing, wood products, tobacco, and chemicals.

Indonesia exports plywood, rubber, sugar, tobacco, palm oil, coffee, tea, **cacao**, textiles, clothing, and footwear. Major imports include consumer goods, raw materials, and fuels.

Above: Tourism is an important industry in Indonesia. Tourists flock to Bali's beautiful beaches every year.

People and Lifestyle

More than 300 **ethnic** groups live in Indonesia, including people from China, Malaysia, Borneo, Thailand, and other Asian countries. Over 250 languages are spoken in the archipelago. Minority groups include the Chinese, the Dutch, and the Vietnamese.

All Indonesians value discipline and self-control. These values are reflected in the art of *batik* (BAH-tik), making

Below:
These women in Bali are dressed in traditional Balinese clothing to attend a temple festival.

Left: This Dani tribesman and his daughter are from Irian Jaya. They are dressed in the traditional style of their tribe. The Dani tribe has not been influenced by modern civilization.

designs that require great patience, as well as in traditional Indonesian dances, which require mental and physical discipline.

Indonesia's Relocation Program

In 1950, the government started a program to help poor families in overpopulated areas start new lives, with land and houses, in less crowded regions. Over six million Indonesians have been relocated since 1950.

Rural Villages

In **rural** areas of Indonesia, families live and work together. Entire villages are invited to celebrations, and everyone helps prepare and pay for the feasts.

Above: People in rural areas bathe and wash their clothes in river water.

In rural homes, young couples and grandparents often live together. A typical village home is built on stilts that raise it 10 to 12 feet (3 to 3.6 m) off the ground. People get into their homes by climbing a ladder. The ladder is removable to keep out unwanted guests.

City Life

Like rural villagers, city dwellers usually live near their relatives. Average working families live in small apartments. Poorer families live in tin and cardboard shacks at the edge of a city.

Young adults take care of their parents and grandparents, so apartments in the cities can be quite crowded. In some apartment complexes, kitchens, bathrooms, and some appliances, such as televisions and washing machines, are shared by many households.

Above: The three-wheeled rickshaw is a common form of transportation in Yogyakarta. Many of these rickshaws are colorfully decorated.

Education

The Dutch did not develop a system of education in Indonesia during their colonial rule. Public education in Indonesia was established only in 1947. At that time, about 80 percent of Indonesians aged fifteen and above could not read or write. Today, Indonesia has many schools. Primary education is required, and it is free. The quality of educational facilities, however, still needs improvement.

Above: Indonesian children attend a primary school for six years.

Only about 10 percent of the students who apply to Indonesia's public universities are admitted. Students who are not admitted may attend private schools, if they can afford them. The oldest university in Indonesia is Gadjah Mada University in Yogyakarta. Indonesian students frequently go to foreign universities, too, especially those in the United States, Australia, and the Netherlands.

Below: These Muslim schoolgirls in South Celebes are returning home after a day of classes.

Religion

The Indonesian people belong to many religions. In 1945, Sukarno introduced the Pancasila (pan-cah-SEE-lah), or Five Principles, for religious guidance. The Pancasila teaches people, whether Muslim, Hindu, Christian, or Buddhist, to believe in one supreme god.

Islam

In the ninth century, Arab and Malay spice traders brought Islam to Indonesia. Many Indonesians adopted Islam because they liked its teaching that all people are equal. Today, most Indonesians are Muslims.

Above: During Ramadan, the Muslims' month of **fasting**, Muslim women wear long white gowns when they pray.

Other Religions

Christians are the second largest religious group in Indonesia. They make up about 9 percent of the population. About 2 percent of the population is Hindu. Most of the Hindus live on the island of Bali. Among other faiths, about 1.6 million Indonesians are Buddhist. The world's largest Buddhist monument, named Borobudur, is in Indonesia.

Below: Melasti is a Hindu purification ceremony that is celebrated three days before the Balinese New Year.

Language

The official language of Indonesia is *Bahasa* (bah-HAH-sah) *Indonesia*. It came from ***pasar Malay*** (pah-sahr mah-lay), or market Malay, a language used by traders in the colonial period, which contained Chinese, Dutch, English, and Indian elements. Malay was chosen as the basis for an official national language because it was the language most widely used when Indonesia became independent. Other languages are Javanese, Madurese, and Sundanese.

Left: Throughout Indonesia, a wide selection of magazines and newspapers are sold at newsstands.

Written literature in Java dates back to the great Hindu epics of the tenth century. After World War I, literature flourished in Indonesia. The earliest Indonesian novels were written in the 1920s. Important writers of that time included Sanuse Pane and Idrus. Chairil Anwar was one of Indonesia's most outstanding modern poets.

Arts

Indonesians are very creative people, and art is a major part of their lives. It plays an important role in many festivals and religious ceremonies.

The many groups that came to Indonesia over the centuries have strongly influenced its culture. Hindus and Buddhists might have had the greatest influence.

Left: One of the most famous Indonesian dances is the *legong* (LAY-gong), which originated in Bali. It is a graceful dance, usually performed by young girls wearing ornate costumes and headdresses.

Music and Dance

The traditional dances of Java and Bali are based on Hindu stories, such as the *Ramayana* and the *Mahabharata*. The most famous dances in Indonesia include the legong, *kecak* (ke-chak), and *barong* (BAH-rong). *Gamelan* (gah-MAY-lahn) orchestras usually provide the music for Indonesian dance performances.

Wayang

Shadow puppet shows, or ***wayang*** (wah-yahng), are popular in Indonesia. Forms of this art include *wayang kulit* (wah-yahng koo-lit), which uses leather puppets, and *wayang golek* (wah-yahng goh-lek), with wooden puppets.

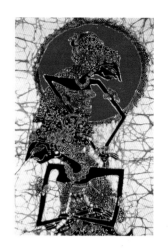

Above: Shadow puppets are a common **motif** in art forms such as batik.

Textiles

One of the most fascinating art forms in Indonesia is batik, which creates

Above: Indonesian art often features scenes from daily life or dancers in elaborate costumes.

patterned fabrics using melted wax and colored dyes. Batik designs originated in Java many centuries ago.

Another unique art form is *ikat* (EE-kaht), which means "tie." Ikat is the process of dyeing threads before they are woven into patterned cloth. One piece of ikat can take over a year to complete. Some artists weave gold and silver threads through cloth to produce fabrics that are used to make formal clothing and costumes for dancers.

Above: Indonesian art often features scenes from daily life or dancers in elaborate costumes.

Opposite: Many Indonesians weave cloth for a living. This woman is weaving on a traditional loom.

Leisure

Indonesians like to watch television, especially local soap operas and programs from the United States. Wayang performances are also popular. Entire villages sometimes gather to watch them.

People who live in Jakarta often spend time shopping, watching movies, and visiting friends and relatives. The schools in Jakarta offer sports and

Below:
On national and school holidays, families crowd the beaches for a day of fun in the sun.

many other after-school activities for students. Young Indonesians also enjoy reading.

Above: Fishing boats in Bali have distinctive triangular sails.

Millions of tourists visit Indonesia's beach resorts every year. Indonesian families often spend their holidays and vacations at the beaches, too. Besides the usual swimming and picnicking, beaches and resorts offer a variety of outdoor activities, such as scuba diving, waterskiing, and jet boating.

Sports

Badminton is a favorite sport in Indonesia. Indonesian players, such as Joko Suprianto and Susi Susanti, held the top worldwide rankings in this sport throughout the 1990s.

Soccer is also popular in Indonesia. The national soccer team won a gold medal in the Southeast Asian (SEA) Games, both in 1987 and 1991.

Above: Rudy Hartono is one of Indonesia's best-known badminton players. He won the All-England Badminton Championship eight times.

Left: Badminton champion Susi Susanti won a gold medal at the 1992 Olympics. She is considered the world's best female badminton player.

Traditional Indonesian sports include *sepak takraw* (SE-pak TAH-kraw), which is similar to volleyball, and stone-jumping. Men on Nias Island used to jump over high stone walls as part of their **initiation** into manhood.

Left: Traditionally, warriors on Nias Island were trained in the dangerous sport of stone-jumping. They had to jump over enemy walls holding a torch in one hand and a weapon in the other.

Festivals

Major festivals in Indonesia honor religious traditions or historical events.

The most important Buddhist festival is Waisak Day. Celebrated on May 25, it **commemorates** the birth, death, and **enlightenment** of Buddha.

Galungan is a ten-day celebration on the island of Bali. It honors the spirits of departed ancestors and is celebrated with prayers and offerings of ripened bananas.

Left: School-children are carrying Indonesian flags in an Independence Day parade.

Muslims celebrate the birth of Prophet Muhammad, the founder of Islam, in a week-long celebration in or near the month of June. Yogyakarta has the largest celebration, with a gamelan performance, a parade of floats, and other activities.

Indonesia celebrates Independence Day on August 17. In Jakarta, a presidential parade and a citizens' march highlight the festivities.

Above: Indonesians dress in traditional clothing for the Lake Toba Festival, which is held in Sumatra.

Food

The cooking techniques of ethnic groups from China, Japan, India, Thailand, and the Netherlands have influenced Indonesian foods.

Favorite Indonesian dishes include *satay* (sah-tay), cubes of meat grilled on sticks and dipped in a spicy peanut sauce, and *soto ayam* (soh-toh EYE-yahm), chicken soup served with

Below: Satay is roasted over burning coals. It is usually served with cucumbers, onions, and *ketupat* (ke-too-paht), or rice cakes.

chunks of chicken, cabbage, bean sprouts, noodles, and fried potatoes. Other popular foods are *nasi goreng* (nah-see go-reng), fried rice with chicken or shrimp and chili, and *gado gado* (GAH-doh GAH-doh), a vegetable salad with peanut sauce.

Indonesians enjoy mangoes, durian, and other tropical fruits. Durian is known as the "king of the fruits." It is creamy white or yellow inside and has spiky, green skin.

INDONESIA

SOUTH CHINA SEA

1

●Banda Aceh

Medan
Mount Sinabung
(8,038 ft / 2,450 m)

Lake Toba

Nias

Bukittinggi●

Sumatra

M A L A Y S I A

SINGAPORE

BRUNEI

**Sabah
(MALAYSIA)**

**Sarawak
(MALAYSIA)**

B o r n e o

2

Ketapang●

Kalimantan

Bengkulu●

Palembang●

*INDIAN
OCEAN*

JAKARTA

Java

Surabaya●

Madura

Yogyakarta●

Mount Bromo
(7,848 ft / 2,392 m)

Bali

Mount Agung
10,308 ft / 3,142 m)

3

State Boundary
Provincial Boundary
Equator
Capital
City
River

42

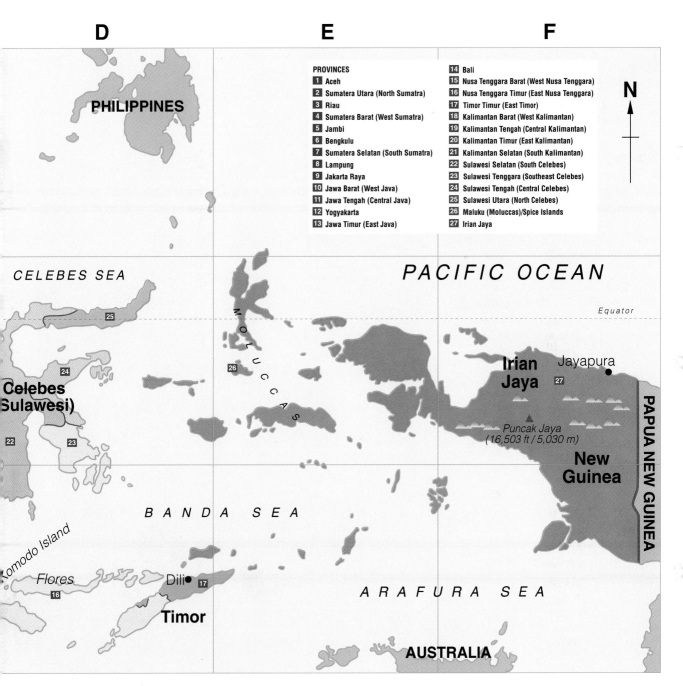

D

E

F

PHILIPPINES

N

CELEBES SEA

PACIFIC OCEAN

Equator

M O L U C C A S

25

26

24

Celebes
(Sulawesi)

22

23

Irian
Jaya

Jayapura

27

Puncak Jaya
(16,503 ft / 5,030 m)

New
Guinea

PAPUA NEW GUINEA

B A N D A   S E A

Komodo Island

Flores

16

Dili

17

Timor

A R A F U R A   S E A

AUSTRALIA

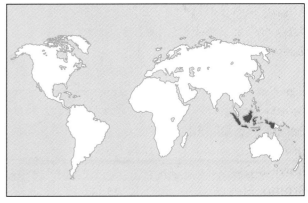

Quick Facts

Official Name Republic of Indonesia

Capital Jakarta

Official Language Bahasa Indonesia

Population 216,108,345 (July 1999 estimate)

Land Area 741,052 square miles (1,919,325 square km)

Major Islands Borneo (Kalimantan), Celebes, Java, the Moluccas, New Guinea (Irian Jaya), Sumatra

Highest Point Puncak Jaya 16,503 feet (5,030 m)

Largest Lake Toba 442 square miles (1,145 square km)

Provinces Aceh, Bali, Bengkulu, Irian Jaya, Jakarta Raya, Jambi, Jawa Barat, Jawa Tengah, Jawa Timur, Kalimantan Barat, Kalimantan Selatan, Kalimantan Tengah, Kalimantan Timur, Lampung, Maluku, Nusa Tenggara Barat, Nusa Tenggara Timur, Riau, Sulawesi Selatan, Sulawesi Tengah, Sulawesi Tenggara, Sulawesi Utara, Sumatera Barat, Sumatera Selatan, Sumatera Utara, Timor Timur, Yogyakarta

Currency Rupiah (8,396.98 rupiah = U.S. $1 in 2000)

Opposite: Jakarta, the capital of Indonesia, is one of the world's most populated cities.

Glossary

archipelago: a chain of islands.

bajaj (BAH-jaj): a small car with three wheels used for public transportation.

batik (BAH-tik): patterned fabric made by waxing and dyeing cloth.

cacao: the seeds of a tropical evergreen tree that are used to make chocolate and cocoa.

commemorates: remembers or calls to mind.

constitutional republic: a government based on written laws and headed by a president who is elected by the people.

corrupt: willing to be dishonest or to do something illegal in return for money.

dictator: a ruler who has complete authority over a country.

enlightenment: the term used in some religions, such as Buddhism, to mean "understanding the true nature of the world."

ethnic: relating to a certain race or culture of people.

fasting: not eating at certain times or for certain periods of time, especially for religious reasons.

gamelan (gah-MAY-lahn): a type of Indonesian orchestra that uses drums, gongs and other kinds of percussion instruments.

initiation: the acts or ceremonies through which a person becomes a member of a group.

investors: people who give or lend their money to support a business, expecting to receive in return a share of what the business earns.

kecak (ke-chak): a Balinese dance in which the dancers go into a trance.

monsoon: a strong, seasonal wind.

motif: a pattern or design that follows a theme and is usually repeated.

ousted: removed or expelled from a place or position.

pasar Malay (pah-sahr mah-lay): the informal Malay language on which the official language of Indonesia is based.

pungent: unpleasantly sharp or bitter.

recession: a period during which the economy of a country becomes very weak.

rural: relating to the countryside.

sepak takraw (SE-pak TAH-kraw): a game similar to volleyball, played with a ball that is made of cane or plastic.

wayang (wah-yahng): dramas performed using shadow puppets.

More Books to Read

The Dancing Pig. Judy Sierra
(Gulliver Books)

Indonesia (Ticket To). Robin Lim
(Carolrhoda Books)

Indonesia. Faces and Places series.
Patrick Ryan (Child's World)

Indonesia. Festivals of the World series.
Elizabeth Berg (Gareth Stevens)

Indonesia. Major World Nations series.
Gary Lyle (Chelsea House)

Indonesia in Pictures. Tom Gerst, editor
(Lerner)

*Komodo Dragons: Giant Lizards
of Indonesia.* James Martin
(Capstone)

Pak in Indonesia. My Future series.
Alain Cheneviere (Lerner)

Rice is Life. Rita Golden Gelman
(Henry Holt)

*Volcanoes, Betjaks, and 'Dragons':
Let's Travel to Indonesia Together.
Windows on the World* series.
Jeannette P. Windham (Global
Age Publishing)

Videos

*Borneo and Indonesia/Australia and New
Zealand. Full Circle with Michael
Palin* (vol. 3). (PBS Home Video)

Experience Indonesia. (Lonely Planet)

Indonesia: Jeweled Archipelago.
(IVN Entertainment)

*The Search for Indonesia's Most Secret
Animal.* (United American Video)

Web Sites

discover-indo.tierranet.com

www.bali-paradise.com/bali/index.html

www.interknowledge.com/indonesia

www.pacificnet.net/gamelan/wayang.html

Due to the dynamic nature of the Internet, some web sites stay current longer than others. To find additional web sites, use a reliable search engine with one or more of the following keywords to help you locate information about Indonesia. Keywords: *Bali, batik, gamelan, Indonesians, Jakarta, Suharto, Sukarno, wayang, Yogyakarta.*

Index